JOHN MARTIN
SKETCHES OF MY LIFE

JOHN MARTIN
SKETCHES OF MY LIFE

Edited and with an Introduction by
Martin Myrone

Tate Publishing

First published 2011 by order of the Tate Trustees
by Tate Publishing, a division of Tate Enterprises Ltd,
Millbank, London SW1P 4RG
www.tate.org.uk/publishing

A catalogue record for this book is available
from the British Library

ISBN 978 1 85437 928 3

Designed by Rose
Reproduction by DL Imaging Ltd, London
Printed in Slovenia by DZS Grafik
Printed on sustainably sourced, certified paper

Cover: John Martin, *Joshua Commanding the
Sun to Stand Still upon Gibeon* 1848 (detail, fig.1)
Frontispiece: Charles Martin, *John Martin on
his Deathbed* 1854, chalk on paper
58.5 × 45.5 cm. Laing Art Gallery,
Tyne & Wear Archives & Museums

Photo credits: Courtesy Kirklees Council (cover
and fig.1); Tyne & Wear Archives & Museums
(frontispiece); Tate Photography © Tate 2010
(fig.2); Courtesy John Weedy www.iln.org.uk (fig.3);
© The Trustees of the British Museum (figs.4, 5)

INTRODUCTION
Martin Myrone

During February and March 1849, the popular weekly newspaper the *Illustrated London News* featured a series of reports on the newly opened exhibition of contemporary art at the British Institution in Pall Mall, in central London. Aimed at respectable, middle-class, family orientated readers around the country, the *Illustrated London News* commented on and illustrated exhibitions and public displays in the context of its very broad coverage of domestic and international news, culture, sport and society gossip.[1] Among the engravings illustrating pictures that year was a reproduction of a large painting of an epic biblical subject, *Joshua Commanding the Sun to Stand Still upon Gibeon* (fig.1), by a senior figure in British art, John Martin (1789–1854), which featured prominently in the exhibition (and is now in the Charles Brooke Crawshaw Collection in Dewsbury Town Hall).[2] Dwelling on this picture, the reviewer ventured a biographical notice of the painter, the inaccuracies of which prompted Martin to write to the editor, John Timbs (1801–1875), offering his own autobiographical notes and hoping to set the record straight. Published in the next issue (17 March), this is the fullest statement about his life made by the artist, giving an exceptional insight into the artist's self-perception and public persona. It is this letter, much-quoted in later accounts as the artist's 'autobiography', which is reprinted here, together with materials from the offending review.

The review, containing some errors of fact regarding Martin's early life and its limited praise for the artist's latest production, is unsigned, and it has been proposed that the author was the prolific writer Peter Cunningham (1816–1869). As he had married the painter's second daughter, Zenobia, in 1842, and was therefore Martin's son-in-law, we would expect that he might have been better informed.[3] Whoever the author, the very fact that Martin was prompted to deliver this autobiographical missive, as a response to a newspaper review which, as Timbs claimed defensively in an editorial note, featured errors that 'are neither numerous nor important', may be telling in itself. Martin had, in fact, been prompted to deliver such a letter once before, when in 1834 he wrote to the art journal the *Athenaeum* to refute misunderstandings about his relationship with the American painter Washington Allston (1779–1843), who was generally suspected of having originated the idea for Martin's most famous single picture, *Belshazzar's Feast* (1820; private collection).[4] But this later letter is longer, fuller, and is obviously able to cover more of his life (even though Martin apparently simply runs out of space and feels compelled to compress his account of 'the last twenty years').

Coming from a humble background in Northumbria, and training not as a fine artist but as a decorative painter, Martin struggled to become integrated into the metropolitan art world when he moved to London in 1806. Forced to make a living working as a china-painter and drawing master, he was led to produce paintings whose novelty and sensational effects would secure the public's attention, even if he lacked reputation and connections in the art world. Although he achieved unprecedented public acclaim for the large paintings of biblical catastrophe and natural disaster that he exhibited in the late 1810s and 1820s, much of the art establishment and the majority of serious-minded critics remained at best sceptical about, and sometimes openly hostile towards, his art. He was never elected a member of the Royal Academy of Arts, London's leading art institution, as might have been expected of any artist of his public prominence. Martin was, in the fullest sense of the term, a commercial artist, whose images were geared towards a mass audience for art, and who needed to make money from his paintings and prints. Martin's dedication to printmaking, and his execution of repetitions of key compositions, suggest his interest in making the most of his original inventions. And whilst the Royal Academy had a rule against artists showing the same composition at its exhibitions more than once, Martin often used alternative exhibition spaces (notably that of the British Institution) to reshow works. His efforts at maximising his artistic investments were, however, frequently undermined by piracy, plagiarism, and commercial exploitation, which made him acutely

1
Joshua Commanding the Sun to Stand Still upon Gibeon 1848
Oil on canvas 148 × 246 cm
Huddersfield Art Gallery, Kirklees Collection (Dewsbury Town Hall), Kirklees Council

conscious of his public image and the need to manage his reputation. He was aware, too, of how his art was constantly compared to works by other painters who had a more conventional painting style, and more official recognition, and how he was perceived by many contemporary commentators as being overlooked by, and perhaps in return antagonistic towards, the art establishment. For example, Francis Danby (1793–1861), who in the 1820s had successfully established himself as a painter of sublime landscapes to rival Martin, had been an Associate of the Royal Academy since 1825. In 1849 he exhibited a large and atmospheric picture at the British Institution that was paired by the critics with Martin's *Joshua*. The painter William Bell Scott (1811–90) recalled that 'Danby ... had perhaps the actual advantage of a more skilful command of the palette, and he had the accidental advantage of being taken up, in opposition to Martin, by the Academy.'[5]

For Martin, the misrepresentation of his life and work, as he saw it, came at a particularly sensitive time. In March 1849 he was probably still completing a rather hastily executed new picture, illustrating the popular poem *King Arthur* by an old admirer of his, Edward Bulwer-Lytton (1803–1873), published the year before. The finished painting, *Arthur and Aegle in the Happy Valley* (Laing Art Gallery, Newcastle) was a characteristic effort towards securing general attention, given the considerable popular interest in the source material.[6] It was also in 1849 that he wrote to Lord Robert Grosvenor (1801–1893) complaining that his 'exertions for the public good had hitherto proved serious inroads on his finances, and were likely to reduce him to still greater difficulties if some compensation was not speedily made'.[7] These 'exertions' were the various ambitious proposals for metropolitan improvement that had much occupied Martin since the late 1820s, and which he takes the opportunity to catalogue in his autobiographical letter. These had been a huge drain on his finances and his energies, and had long distracted him from the practice of painting. The spectacular artistic successes he had scored in the 1820s were behind him, and if these had been followed by the critical and popular triumph of his mezzotint illustrations to Milton and the Bible, by the end of the 1830s Martin was plunged into personal and financial crisis. He had made a recovery of sorts when he returned to painting, using a project in 1838–9 to paint Queen Victoria's coronation to make contact with potential patrons (in which effort he had some success). But although he exhibited and indeed sold several major canvases in the 1840s, he was more often to exhibit modest landscapes and watercolours at the London exhibitions. Accordingly, his critical reputation remained by 1849 fragile, his financial circumstances unstable.

If Martin was sensitive about his monetary situation and his perceived exclusion from the art establishment, the *Illustrated London News* article was destined to cause offence. With a degree of romantic exaggeration that its subject found unacceptable, the biography outlines the artist's humble background in the north of England, his artisanal training, his precarious existence in London, and the series of popular pictures he showed at exhibition in the later 1810s and 1820s. The report goes to some length to argue that Martin sold himself short in the following years, as he failed to capitalise on this initial success and exhibited a series of substandard works. Thus is explained Martin's failure to be elected as a member of the Royal Academy, with the implication that he displayed some degree of haughtiness. In response, Martin was at pains to point out that his disagreement was 'not with individual members' but rather the monopolistic basis of the Academy as an institution.

But there was more at stake than professional manners. For the writer in the *Illustrated London News*, as for other reviewers of the time, *Joshua* represented something of a return to form for Martin. It was, unusually, a second full-scale version of a picture that had first been seen by London exhibition-goers more than thirty years earlier. The original *Joshua* was a surprise hit at the annual exhibition of the Royal Academy in London 1816, helping to establish Martin's name as a painter of a novel form of historical and sublime landscapes. As Martin notes, he was awarded a cash prize by the British Institution when it was exhibited there the following year, but its later history was more troubling to the painter. In 1821, Martin secured even greater public acclaim when his *Belshazzar's Feast* was shown at the British Institution. While the picture was on show, Martin sold it and *Joshua* to his former employer, the glass-painter William Collins (c.1780–c.1840) for 800 guineas. Collins toured the pictures around provincial gallery spaces relentlessly through the 1820s. In 1826 he applied for an injunction against Martin, after the artist announced plans to publish a print of the composition. Collins claimed that he bought the picture 'with a view to print and publish Engravings', and Martin had signed a contract engaging 'to permit no duplicate, copy or sketch of the large picture of Belshazzar's Feast until you have disposed of the same'.[8] Although the injunction does not seem to have been imposed as Martin produced his print, the fact that Collins was able to claim his commercial rights over an image originated by the painter was a source of aggravation. The issue of an artist's right to exploit commercially his own productions exercised Martin throughout his career, something that he alludes to in his autobiography when he refers to 'the imperfect laws of copyright' leading to 'my property being so constantly and variously infringed'.

The reappearance of the original *Joshua* in 1848, when it was sold to the Liverpool businessman John Naylor (1813–1889), provided the occasion for revisiting the composition. The repainting of this composition, itself was, as much as the autobiography, an opportunity for Martin to revisit and revise his personal history. In 1848 he claimed that he had not seen the original picture for twenty years, something that was 'an annoyance to him' and that the new version is 'a commission from a gentleman who greatly admired the design of the original'.[9] This 'gentleman' was Charles Scarisbrick (1800–1860), a very wealthy landowner and businessman who became famously reclusive and eccentric. He had inherited Scarisbrick Hall in Lancashire in the 1830s, putting the pioneering architect and designer A.N.W. Pugin (1812–1852) to work remodelling it as an opulent and extensive Gothic revival mansion. In the autobiography Martin counts Scarisbrick as among his 'recent' patrons, and singles him out for his generosity. Scarisbrick eventually owned twenty-four pictures by the artist, which were dispersed by sale in 1861 after his death. Besides being the single most extensive collector of Martin's works, he collected Old Master paintings and medieval carvings, and was a prolific purchaser of what we would today term architectural salvage.[10] Quite how Martin's paintings sat with the dark mock-medieval interiors of the Hall and the rest of Scarisbrick's collection is hard to ascertain, though architectural historian Mark Girouard's reference to this setting as 'an antiquary's hide out, a glorified junk box put together with jackdaw rather than connoisseur enthusiasm' is suggestive.[11] What we do know is that Scarisbrook was a Catholic, and as such still likely to be viewed as an 'outsider' by the British establishment. He was also fantastically hard-nosed in his business dealings (he had secured the ownership of the Scarisbrick estate only after taking his own sisters to court). Although a landowner, he was also deeply involved in industrial investments of one sort or another, including the railways, coal mining, brick making, stone quarrying, and property speculation.[12]

Naylor and Scarisbrick represent precisely the kind of regionally based industrial wealth that the critic of the *Illustrated London News* points to as a new patron of art in his introductory remarks to the review of the 1849 British Institution show: 'the manufacturers of Manchester, Leeds, Liverpool, Bradford, and Birmingham, [who] vie with the nobility in the acquisition of works of art, and pay, at times, even more liberally for what they want'. The reviewer pitches this new breed of patron against the aristocratic and metropolitan connoisseurs of an earlier era, the people who had, pointedly, originally established the British Institution as an alternative to the artist-run Royal Academy. Their patronage has, the reviewer is suggesting, been displaced. We can detect here the rise of a distinct 'middle class' taste for art, which was opposed (perhaps militantly) to aristocratic traditions. Certainly, it would be hard not to identify in the reviewer's words some deliberate political intent, in the wake of the Chartist petition to Parliament in 1848 with its assertion of the rights of ordinary people against aristocratic privilege.

Even in the limited context of the *Illustrated London News* itself, we can see the review and Martin's response participating in a news culture that is determinedly middle-class, commercialised, and also, importantly, global in its outlook. Martin's autobiographical letter featured in an issue where the main story was 'Local and General Taxation' together with an illustration and report on the carnival in Rome, accompanied by sections on 'Foreign and Colonial News', 'The Theatres', 'Railway Intelligence', an illustrated account of the exhibition of 'Recent British Manufactures' at the Society of Arts and the fourth notice of the exhibition of the British Institution (followed by Martin's letter), reports on parliamentary proceedings, the regular column on chess, obituaries, sports and racing news, a page of advertisements ('Does your Hair Fall Off or Get Grey?' ... 'Emigration Facilitated' ... 'Patent Galvanic Pens' ... 'Breidenbach's Amandine, for Whitening the Hands', and so forth) and eyewitness sketches of a 'Settler's Hut ... an Australian dwelling of a class commonly met with in the Bush', among much else. If discussion of art had expanded in the eighteenth century to encompass 'coffee house culture', and early nineteenth-century literary culture had expanded the sense of culture's value and place in the world, here was art being seen as part of a continuum of news and social affairs.[13] The personal, local, national, and international are connected, together with the commercial and the artistic, the high and the low.

In these various dimensions, the review and letter published in the *Illustrated London News* may point to the emergence of a popular and decidedly non-aristocratic taste for art. But things are not perhaps quite that simple; in his autobiography Martin goes to some lengths to name-check his high-born (and occasionally royal) patrons, and to draw attention to the honours he had received from academies abroad. This suggests a degree of nostalgia, a yearning for older forms of elite patronage, and the repainting of *Joshua* was in itself perhaps a means for him to reassert an old-fashioned form of relationship between the artist and his patron, whereas the destiny of the first painting was to be swallowed up in a distinctly modern form of commercial enterprise that offered little direct benefit to the painter himself. His response to the article in the *Illustrated London News* even suggests that he was not in fact happy to be characterised as an anti-academic outsider; he was not prepared to dismiss art academies as a source of artistic authority. As for the painting of *Joshua*, it was not simply a replica, but a revision of the earlier version of the picture, and was, significantly, much more freely and expressively painted than the original. The painting of 1816 is characterised by cool greys and earth tones, with the landscape and atmospheric effects rendered in restrained detail, and the massed armies minutely painted. The picture of 1849 is grey and silver and blue, punctuated by a few bright figures, with the painted surface itself displaying a degree of breadth and animation not seen in Martin's work before, but characteristic of the work of the most highly admired and experimental of British landscape painters, J.M.W. Turner (1775–1851). Martin's striving for an overall painterly effect may have been simply commercially expedient, being less labour-intensive (the multitude of tiny figures seen in the earlier version are here obscured by the landscape or lost in the atmosphere) but it also struck a note of artistic affect. The critic of the *Illustrated London News* complained that the picture was 'too blue', and several other reviewers commented on the 'cold', 'inky' qualities of the painting.

Taking a different tack, the *Examiner* (17 February 1849) ended its review with a rather terse comment: 'Mr Martin has another "Joshua" which will doubtless have many admirers'. For many critics Martin's sheer popularity was anathema. Which is not to say, however, that his work represents simply a 'popular' (or 'low') taste; he remained, until the end of his life, a painter of easel pictures, pictures that, even if they challenged the limits of conventional taste and were effectively marketed to a mass audience for art, nevertheless worked within the conventions of fine art and dealt with the kind of historic or 'poetical' subjects prescribed by traditional academic art theory. Indeed, Martin's revision of *Joshua* can be interpreted as an effort to make his painting more 'painterly' or 'artistic' in a way that pushed the formal boundaries of art (if only as far as Turner had extended those boundaries several decades earlier). As the reviewer of the *Illustrated London News* noted, 'as a whole it is *better* and more firmly painted than is usual with Mr Martin's light and facile pencil'. A common complaint directed against his earlier pictures by critics was that they were formally diffuse, consisting of a repetitious, improbable overloading of details, without the kind of unified pictorial organisation and legible spatial structure expected of paintings. The writer Charles Lamb (1775–1834), one of Martin's most outspoken critics, complained of the original Joshua that it is 'a confused piece ... frittered into 1000 pieces, little armies here, little armies there – you should see only the *Sun* and Joshua'.[14] The painterly breadth of the new

2
The Last Judgement 1853
Oil on canvas 196.8 × 225.8 cm
Tate

Joshua, which together with compositional adjustments serves to obscure the 'little armies', might be interpreted as a response to such criticism, displaying a distinctly 'middlebrow', even gauche, reverence for the forms of legitimate culture (in this case, 'firmer', more painterly, 'fine art'). What we may see in these critical and artistic revisions is the negotiation of a distinctly modern (and distinctly unstable, endlessly disputable and subjective) division between the 'highbrow' and the 'middlebrow': the former being intellectually challenging, difficult or uncomfortable, and therefore capable of appreciation only by the minority, the latter adopting elevated forms but in an undemanding, accessible, and characteristically belated way.[15]

Given the apocalyptic extravagance of his most famous pictures (see fig.2), it is tempting to place Martin in a lineage of compulsive visionaries or religiously inspired eccentrics, and to cast him as the victim of a conservative art world or as a passionate outsider who anticipates the excesses of modern popular culture. Yet Martin's religious views were never clearly expressed, and the characteristics that his closest contemporaries noted of him concerned his dandyism, personal warmth, his energy and his scientific interests and rationalism. Writing to Martin's daughter Isabella shortly after the artist's death in 1854, Scarisbrick could remark: 'I can well believe he viewed the approach of Death calmly & without fear – for he had trained himself to a constant contemplation of the great changes of Creation & Life – and had penetrated as far as the imagination ever can, the hidden mysteries of the future.'[16] Martin is here presented as a visionary, perhaps, but also a calm rationalist and – strikingly – occupied with the contemplation of the grand cycles of nature and history rather than a feverishly inspired spirituality. These are comments that should make us question our perceptions of Martin, his beliefs and artistic expectations, and his place in a developing art world. Accordingly, the 'autobiography' reprinted here may be disappointing to modern eyes, offering little in the way of sensation, and emphasising the author's reasonable character and all-too worldly commercial struggles. But this text, the writing of which must have been prompted by Martin's own self-doubts, his sense of financial and artistic vulnerability, is a rich document of a complex, contradictory life, and, indeed, the complexity and contradictions surrounding 'art' in the emerging modern age of mass-media, democracy and popular entertainment.

NOTES

1   See Peter W. Sinnema, *Dynamics of the Pictured Page: Representing the Nation in the Illustrated London News*, Aldershot 1998, pp.12–14.

2   Robert Hall, *Paintings in Dewsbury Town Hall*, Kirklees Libraries, Museums & Arts 1989. For general studies of Martin, see: Mary Pendered, *John Martin, Painter: His Life and Times*, London 1923; Thomas Balston, *John Martin 1789–1854: His Life and Works*, London 1947; William Feaver, *The Art of John Martin*, Oxford 1975.

3   The identification of Cunningham as the author of the original review was ventured by Mary Pendered, the first modern writer on Martin, and had been gleaned from private correspondence with Cunningham's own son, W.A. Cunningham (1850–1936) (Pendered 1923, pp.37, 259). He had told Pendered that his father had been busy as a writer on the *Illustrated London News*, 'contributing a weekly article headed "Town and Table Talk on Literature and Art"'. Cunningham was known as a prolific contributor to periodicals, and it seemed feasible that he was the author of that review. However, the commentary of 1849 appeared under its own heading as an exhibition review, and the column 'Town Talk and Table Talk' to which Cunningham did contribute and which his son was presumably recalling did not start until 1850. Although Pendered's claim has been repeated in the modern literature, the attribution is therefore by no means certain.

4   *Athenaeum*, 14 June 1834, p.459.

5   William Bell Scott, *Our British Landscape Painters* (1872), quoted in Eric Adams, *Francis Danby: Varieties of Poetic Landscape*, New Haven and London 1973, p.79.

6   However, the picture was poorly received at exhibition that year and Bulwer-Lytton failed to buy it, as Martin had hoped, even though he offered it to him for a knock-down price. See the letters from Martin to Bulwer-Lytton of April and May 1849 in Hertfordshire Record Office, DE/K/C11/33–34.

7   Quoted in Balston 1947, p.128.

8   National Archives, Kew, C13/2017/22.

9   John Martin to James Palmer, 9 December 1848, Naylor Papers, Walker Art Gallery, Liverpool, 14a.

10   Mark Girouard, *The Victorian Country House*, revised edn, New Haven and London 1979, pp.110–19; John Harris, *Moving Rooms: The Trade in Architectural Salvage*, New Haven and London 2007, pp.49–51.

11   Girouard 1979, p.115.

12   John K. Walton, *Lancashire: A Social History 1558–1939*, Manchester 1987, p.128.

13   On the early nineteenth-century expansion of the sense of cultural enfranchisement, see 'Introducing Romantic Sociability' in Gillian Russell and Clara Tuite (eds.), *Romantic Sociability: Social Networks and Literary Culture in Britain 1770–1840*, Cambridge 2002, pp.1–23, esp. p.19.

14   Charles Lamb to Bernard Barton, 11 June 1827, in E.V. Lucas (ed.), *The Letters of Charles Lamb*, 3 vols., London 1935, vol.1, pp.97–8.

15   See Erica Brown, 'Introduction' to papers from the conference 'Investigating the Middlebrow' (Sheffield Hallam University, 2007) <http://extra.shu.ac.uk/wpw/middlebrow/Brown.html>

16   Charles Scarisbrick to Isabella Martin, 22 February 1854, Cambridge University Library, Department of Manuscripts and University Archives, MS Add. 9389/5/S/2.

EXTRACTS FROM THE
ILLUSTRATED LONDON NEWS
17 February – 17 March 1849

INCLUDING
JOHN MARTIN'S AUTOBIOGRAPHY

Illustrated London News, 17 February 1849, pages 104–5

OPENING OF THE BRITISH INSTITUTION EXHIBITION

The first exhibition of pictures of the London season, in point of time, is invariably the collection at the British Institution. It announces April, May, and the usual period of the London season, much better than the Almanack, or Term Time at Westminster Hall, and is a fair rival, in its seasonable looks, to Covent Garden market. It has always been a popular Exhibition, nor will this, its three-and-thirtieth, we believe, tend to lessen its popularity, or abridge its usefulness.[1] It is true, indeed, that the Exhibition, viewed as a whole, is hardly up to a level of its earlier displays; but it is more than an average Exhibition, and contains many pleasing pictures. The complaint which we have heard, and seen even in print, that only one Royal Academician is an exhibitor, is rather a cheering circumstance in the history of art, for it must be remembered that the British Institution was established not so much for the *exhibition* as for the *sale* of the works of art, and the purchasers of pictures are now one hundred times as numerous as they were when the Institution was founded, in 1805. We have plenty of Sir George Beaumonts now, and it has become almost an impossibility that another picture, of equal merit to Wilkie's "Blind Fiddler," should be sold again for so insignificant a sum as fifty guineas.[2] When the Institution was founded, almost the only purchasers of pictures were the nobility and gentry resident in London. Now it is very different; the manufacturers of Manchester, Leeds, Liverpool, Bradford, and Birmingham, vie with the nobility in the acquisition of works of art, and pay, at times, even more liberally for what they want …

The present collection consists of 514 pictures, and 14 pieces of sculpture, contributed by 356 different artists … Mr Martin contributes a large picture of "Joshua commanding the Sun to stand still," a commission, we believe, from a well-known patron of British art.[3] The incidents and combination of effect are the same as in the large engraving, but the painting is certainly superior to anything which we remember to have seen from Mr Martin's easel for several years.[4] The distances are admirably managed, and the whole conception brought out in a most wonderful manner. It is perhaps a little too blue.[5]

Illustrated London News, 24 February 1849, page 121

EXHIBITION OF THE BRITISH INSTITUTION. SECOND NOTICE

In the History and Subject department, Mr Martin leads the way with his "Joshua commanding the Sun to stand still". Mr Danby follows hard at his heels ...[6]

Illustrated London News, 10 March 1849, page 153 (from pages 152–4)

THE BRITISH INSTITUTION (THIRD NOTICE)

We have taken our illustrations for this week's paper from Mr John Martin's large picture of "Joshua commanding the Sun to stand still," and from the two charming subjects by Mr O'Neill – "St Catherine" and "St Cecilia".[7]

Mr John Martin, the celebrated painter of "Joshua commanding the Sun to stand still," "Belshazzar's Feast,"[8] and other noble works, was born at Newcastle-upon-Tyne, in the year 1789. He was apprenticed to a coach-painter; but, disliking the toil of his master's business, redeemed, by the kindness of his own friends and his own exertions, the remainder of his time, and, bidding farewell to his own family, set off to London in a Newcastle collier, with five shillings in his pocket. He soon found

THE BRITISH INSTITUTION.

"JOSHUA COMMANDING THE SUN TO STAND STILL."—PAINTED BY JOHN MARTIN.

"ST. CECILIA."—PAINTED BY H. O'NEIL.

"ST. CATHERINE."—PAINTED BY H. O'NEIL.

employment in this great metropolis of the world; for a lad with active hands and a determination to get on never can be long out of employment in a large city. He worked at first as a coach-painter, and afterwards as a glass-painter, at Collins's, in the Strand, near Temple-bar, and was living in Thanet-place (at the back of Collins's), when he sent his first work, "Landscape – a composition," to the Royal Academy exhibition at Somerset House.[9] In 1812 (he was then in his twenty-third year) he exhibited "Sadak in search of the Waters of Oblivion," the first work which brought him into notice.[10] In 1813 he exhibited "Adam's first Sight of Eve;"[11] in 1814 "Clytie," an illustration of

> All day, all night, in trackless wilds alone,
> She pined and taught the list'ning rocks to moan.[12]

And in 1816, in the ante-room of the Royal Academy, his first sketch of "Joshua commanding the Sun to stand still."[13] The 'Joshua' attracted, as it deserved to do, very great attention, from the new and highly imaginative manner in which the sublime incident in Scripture was sought to be embodied. The Princess Charlotte immediately appointed him her "historical landscape painter," and the picture itself was bought (but before the exhibition, we believe) by Mr Collins, the dealer in glass, with whom Martin was still working when the picture was exhibited.[14] The "Joshua" was followed by "The Bard" from Gray, and by a figure of "Revenge" from Collins's "Ode to the Passions"[15] – neither very successful, and both, in some respects, very injurious to Mr Martin's interests; as they gave occasion to portrait painters within the Academy, and disappointed historical painters without the walls of the Academy, to observe often and openly that the "Joshua" was more the result of an accident – a happy exception, like the celebrated one speech which gave the name of "Single-speech Hamilton" to a generally dull orator.[16] Nor was it till "The Paphian Bower" appeared in 1822, and the "Belshazzar's Feast" in 1824, that this expression began to be less frequently advanced;[17] and the many, who at last judge for themselves, could see extraordinary and original merit in the works of this great painter. Mr Martin has, in some matters, himself to blame for this false and temporary appreciation of his merits. He did not follow up what he had begun so well; and the architectural drawings which he exhibited at the Academy, of Sir Chas. Cockerell's house in Gloucestershire, were, though clever in themselves, infinitely less than the public expected, and almost demanded at his hands.[18] Had the "Belshazzar," or "The Deluge,"[19] or any of those great works for which Mr Martin has a wide and well-deserved reputation, been produced immediately after the "Joshua," the bitter sayings of the envious artists had been unattended to by the public, and Mr Martin must have been elected into the Royal Academy at the earliest vacancy; whereas, disgusted as he has been with the conduct of his brethren in art, he soon withdrew his name from the list of candidates, and was therefore, by the rules of the Academy, ineligible for election. Mr Martin, therefore, never can be a member. Nor are we disposed to regret the want of that honorary appendage to his name, of RA, of which the public hereafter will care so very little. The works of Hogarth, Romney, Blake, Morland, Harlow, Bonington, and Liversege, realise large prices at Christie's, in spite of their names not being graced with academic distinctions;[20] while the appendage of RA can do nothing for Mr Wheatley, RA; Mrs Moser, RA; Mrs Angelica Kauffman, RA; or even for Mr Howard, RA.[21]

The passage in Scripture which Mr Martin has sought to embody in so remarkable and imaginative a manner is as follows :--

And the Lord discomfited them before Israel, and slew them with great slaughter a[t] Gibeon, and chased them along the way that goeth up to Beth-horon, and smote them to Azekah, and unto Makkedah.

And it came to pass, as they fled before Israel, and were in the going-down to Beth-horon, that the Lord cast down great stones from Heaven upon them unto Azekah, and they died: there were more which died with hailstones than they whom the children of Israel slew with the sword.

Then spake Joshua to the Lord, on the day when the Lord delivered up the Amorites before the children of Israel, and he said, in the sight of Israel, Sun, stand thou still upon Gibeon; and thou Moon in the valley of Ajalon.[22]

The grandeur of an incident like this has afforded Mr Martin an ample opportunity for introducing those wonderful effects *in* nature, and almost, we may say, *out* of nature, for which he has been so long unrivalled. The scene he has realised is a very noble one – he brings the event as it were before us, and makes us a spectator of what is going on. The picture from which our Engraving is made has been painted within the last half-year for a well-known patron of art; and though it is, as we have observed in a former notice, somewhat too blue, as a whole it is *better* and more firmly painted than is usual with Mr Martin's light and facile pencil.

John Martin's 'autobiography', published as a letter in the *Illustrated London News*,

17 March 1849, pages 176–7

MR. JOHN MARTIN.
(To the Editor of the *Illustrated London News*.)

Lindsey House, Chelsea, March 14, 1849.

SIR,– Your Journal is so distinguished for the accuracy of its statements, as rarely to present occasion for question; but the article concerning me in your last Number was so unfortunate a tissue of errors from beginning to end, that it can only have the effect of misleading your readers; and I must, therefore, request your insertion of the following particulars, which, however brief, may at least be replied on, and thus supersede the unauthorised sketches of my life which have hitherto appeared.

I was born at a house called the East-land Ends, Haydon Bridge, near Hexham, 19th July, 1789, and received the rudiments of my education at the well-known free-school of that place.[23] Having, from my early years, attempted to draw, and expressed a determination to "be a painter," the question arose "how to turn my desires to profitable account;" and it was ultimately decided to make me a herald painter – in consequence of which, upon the removal of my family to Newcastle, I was, when 14, apprenticed to Wilson, the coach-builder, of that town.[24] I worked with him for a year, in no small degree disgusted at the drudgery which, as junior apprentice, I had to endure, and at not being allowed to practice the higher mysteries of the art; when, just previously to the expiration of the year (from which period I was to have received an increase of pay), one of the senior apprentices told me that my employer would evade payment of the first quarter on the grounds that "I went on trial," and that "it was not in the indentures." As it had been foretold, so it turned out. Upon claiming the increase, I was referred to my articles, and the original sum was tendered. This I indignantly rejected, saying, "What! you're soon beginning then, and mean to serve me the same as you did such an one? but *I* won't submit;" and, turning on my heel, I hastened home. My father highly approved of my conduct – declared that I should not go back – and immediately furnished me with proper drawing materials, the most satisfactory reward I could receive. I worked away to my heart's content for some days; when, at length, while so employed, the town-sergeant came to take me off to the Guildhall to answer charges brought against me by my master. I was dreadfully frightened, the more so as none of my family were within call to accompany me: and, on entering the court, my heart sank at sight of the aldermen, and my master, with lowering face, and his witnesses. I was charged on oath with insolence – having run away – rebellious conduct – and threatening to do a private injury. In reply, I simply stated the facts as they occurred. The witness produced against me proved the correctness of my statement in every particular; and the consequence was a decision in my favour. Turning, then, to my master, I said "You have stated your dissatisfaction with me, and apprehensions of my doing you a private injury: under these circumstances, you can have no objection to returning my indentures." Mr. Wilson was not prepared for this, but the Alderman immediately said, "Yes, Mr. Wilson, you must give the boy his indentures." They were accordingly handed over to me; and I was so overjoyed, that, without waiting longer, I bowed and thanked the Court, and running off to the coach-factory, flourished the indentures over my head, crying, "I've got my indentures, and your master has taken a false oath; and I don't know whether he is not in the pillory by this!" My family were delighted with the spirit I had displayed, and at my emancipation from an occupation they saw as uncongenial, and my father at once took measures to place me under an Italian master of great merit, and some reputation in Newcastle, named Boniface Musso, the father of the celebrated enamel painter, Charles Muss.[25] I remained under his instructions about a year, when Mr. C. Muss, who was settled in London, wished his father to come and reside with him, and M. Musso urged upon my parents the advantage of my accompanying him. After much cogitation, many misgivings on my mother's part, and solemn charges to our friend, it was ultimately agreed that I should join him in London within a few months. I accordingly arrived in London at the beginning of September, 1806; but, unluckily for the lovers of romance, I was not cast upon the wide world in quite such a forlorn and destitute condition as your contributor states; for I had a good outfit – small, though sufficient funds for immediate purposes, notwithstanding my having been robbed of all my loose cash by a poor passenger in the ship – and most important of all, I was placed under the protection of kind and excellent friends. The treatment I experienced from Mr. C. Muss soon satisfied me that he conceived my means to be far more extended than they were; I therefore took an early opportunity of informing him that I had resolved never more to receive pecuniary assistance from my parents, who had already done enough in providing means for establishing me in London; that, as my present resources were not equal to a due recompense for his liberality, I thought it only right to tell him my position. He was pleased with my honourable candour, and saying that he would do all in his power to promote my laudable intentions, immediately undertook to employ me in his glass and china painting establishment in a department where my facility in designing and painting landscape scenes would be very useful; and from this time I supported myself solely by my own exertions, and with advantage to my employers.[26]

After a few months, feeling uncomfortable, owing to some little indifferences with a member of Mr. M's family, I removed from his house in Wynyatt-street, New River-Head, to Adam-street West, Cumberland-place, continuing to work for Mr. Muss' firm during the day, and sitting up at night till two and three o'clock acquiring that knowledge of perspective and architecture which has since been so valuable to me. Here I remained till 1809, when I married,[27] and removed to Northumberland-street, Marylebone, thence to High-street; thence, in 1818, to 30, Allsop-terrace, New-road; and thence after thirty years' residence, to my present abode: and these are the only places in London I have ever lived in.[28] Shortly before my marriage, Mr. Muss's establishment broke up, and those employed in it had the option of seeking independent employment, or following the fortunes of the different members of the firm. I, of course, accompanied my friend, and was subsequently engaged with him in the glass painting, carried on by Mr. Collins, in the Strand,[29] occupying my evenings upon water-colour drawings, and contriving, in odd hours, to paint in oil my first picture ever exhibited ("A Clytie"), which was sent to the Academy in 1810, and rejected for want of room, though not condemned, as I afterwards learnt through Mr. Tresham.[30] I therefore sent it again in 1811, when it was hung in a good situation in the Great Room![31] At the beginning of the following year, having now lost my employment at Collins's, it became indeed necessary to work hard, and, as I was ambitious of fame, I determined on painting a large picture, "Sadak," which was executed in a month.[32] You may easily guess my feelings when I overheard the men who were placing it in the frame disputing as to which was the top of the picture![33] The work, however, though hung in the ante-room of the Royal Academy, received, to my inexpressible delight, a notice in the newspapers, and was eventually sold, under interesting circumstances, to the late Mr. Manning, for 50 guineas.[34] The following year, 1813, I sent "The Expulsion" to the British Institution, and "Adam's first sight of Eve" to the Royal Academy, and was again given a place in the Room![35] My next painting, "Clytie", though a picture which has stood the test of criticism during many years, was in 1814 placed in the ante-room of the Royal Academy.[36] The following year I sent the "Joshua," which was again hidden in the ante-room; the next year, 1817, I sent it to the British Institution, where it attracted great attention, and I was rewarded with the chief premium of the year, £100; but the picture was not sold till some years afterwards, when it went as a companion to the "Belshazzar."[37]

Down to this period I had supported myself and family by pursuing almost every branch of my profession – teaching – painting small oil pictures, glass enamel paintings, water-colour drawings; in fact, the usual tale of a struggling artist's life. I had been so successful with my sepia drawings, that the Bishop of Salisbury, the tutor to the Princess Charlotte, advised me not to risk my reputation by attempting the large picture of "Joshua."[38] As is generally the case in such matters, these well-meant recommendations had no effect; but, at all events the confidence I had in my powers was justified, for the success of my "Joshua" opened a new era to me.

4
Belshazzar's Feast (first steel plate) 1826
Mezzotint and etching 47.2 × 71.6 cm
The British Museum, London

In 1818 I removed to a superior house, and had to devote my time mainly to executing some immediately profitable works;[39] but, in 1819, I produced the "Fall of Babylon," which was second only to the "Belshazzar" in the attention it excited.[40] The following year came "Macbeth," one of my most successful landscapes.[41] Then, in 1821, "Belshazzar's Feast," an elaborate picture, which occupied a year in executing, and which received the premium of £200 from the British Institution.[42] In the next year, 1822, appeared the "Destruction of Herculaneum," another elaborate work.[43] In 1823, the "Seventh Plague," and "Paphian Bower."[44] In 1824 the "Creation," in 1826 the "Deluge," and in 1828 the "Fall of Nineveh."[45] In addition to the above were many smaller pictures, duplicates of some of the above subjects, sketches, and drawings; but the most important of all was my acquiring the art of engraving, and producing the "Illustrations of Milton," designed on the plates (and for which I received 2000 guineas); the "Belshazzar's Feast," the first large steel plate ever engraved in mezzotinto [fig.4]; the "Joshua," and the "Deluge," [fig.5] between the years 1823 and 1828.[46] Thus it will be seen that all my greatest works which have gained me a reputation both at home and abroad, were produced within the eleven years immediately succeeding the first fair exhibition of my "Joshua," and that "the bitter sayings of envious artists" arose from no inertness on my part, whilst the rapid and substantial success which attended my efforts certainly warranted no supposition of any "false and temporary appreciation of my merits." On the contrary, the inferences are all the other way, if we may judge from the fact that, of all my numerous works, I have but one oil-painting in my possession[47] – the earlier works having been purchased by the late Mr. Henry Philip Hope, the Duke of Buckingham, Lord de Tabley, Earl of Durham, Earl Grey, and others; the more recent ones, by the Duke of Sutherland, Prince Albert, and Mr. Scarisbrick – to whose cultivated taste I am as much indebted as to his liberal patronage.[48] The notice and honours I have received from foreign courts arose chiefly from the circulation of my engravings, as only two of my pictures have ever been seen abroad – the "Fall of Nineveh" at Brussels, and the "Deluge" in Paris: the first procured me the large medal of the Exhibition, the Order of Leopold, and my election as a member of the Academy of Antwerp; the second, the gold medal, and a magnificent present of Sèvres from the King of the French.[49] These facts show that if I had enemies amongst the artists, their aspersions did not retard my progress. However, I myself much doubt the existence of such ill-feeling in the outset, though there can be little question that eventually my success, by my own independent means, raised a sufficient number of detractors. As regards the Royal Academy, I, doubtless, had reason to complain; for as I progressed in art and reputation my places on its walls retrograded – my first works being placed in the Great Room, whereas, all the subsequent, and with every show of probability, superior, productions were placed in a dark hole called the Ante-room. This led to my ceasing to enter my name upon its books, to my considering its laws, and to my subsequent opposition on public grounds, my quarrel being, not with individual members, but with the association itself: for I was satisfied what a body so constituted, a close and narrow monopoly, with the privileges of a Royal charter and power of a public institution, could not but produce a mischievous effect on art itself. I have expressed these convictions in evidence before the House of Commons, and yet hope to see a thorough reform, and all such monopolies thrown open.[50]

I have already encroached so much upon your space, that I have scarcely room to account for the last twenty years of my life: suffice it, that some portion was devoted to engraving, which I was eventually obliged to abandon, owing to the imperfect laws of copyright, my property being so constantly and variously infringed, that it became ruinous to contend with those who robbed me; and I was, therefore, driven from the market by inferior copies of my own works, to the manifest injury of my credit and pecuniary resources, while I may, without vanity, affirm, that even art itself suffers by the non-circulation of the engravings, for, of course, neither my own plates nor the pirated copies will sell without the impulse of novelty.[51]

In consequence of the strong interest I have always felt in the improvement of the condition of the people, and the sanitary state of the country, I turned my attention to engineering subjects; and two-thirds of my time, and a very large portion of my pecuniary means, have, since 1827, been devoted to the objects I had at heart, though even here I have been obstructed and injured by the same objection of the inefficiency of the patent laws, and, indeed, total absence of real protection for original designs in engineering and mechanics. Your limits will not admit of the particulars of injuries I have sustained on this head, and I will therefore merely enumerate the plans I have set forth. My attention was first occupied in endeavouring to procure an improved supply of pure water to London, diverting the sewage from the river, and rendering it available as manure; and in 1827 and 1828 I published plans for the purpose.[52] In 1829 I published further plans for accomplishing the same objects by different means, namely, a weir across the Thames, and for draining the marshy lands, &c.[53] In 1832, 1834, 1836, 1838, 1842, 1843, 1845, and 1847, I published and republished additional particulars – being so bent upon my object that I was determined never to abandon it;[54] and though I have reaped no other advantage, I have, at least, the satisfaction of knowing that the agitation thus kept up, constantly, solely by myself, has resulted in a vast alteration in the quantity and quality of water supplied by the companies, and in the establishment of a Board of Health, which will, in all probability, eventually carry out most of the objects I have been so long urging.[55] Amongst the other proposals which I have advanced is my railway connecting the river and docks with all the railways that diverge from London, and apparently approved by the Railway Termini Commissioners, as the line they intimate coincides with that submitted by me, and published in their report[56] – the principle of rail adopted by the Great Western line – the lighthouse for the sands appropriated by Mr. Walker in his Maplin sand lighthouse – the flat anchor and wire cable – mode of ventilating coal-mines – floating harbour and pier – iron ship, and various other inventions of comparatively minor importance, but all conducing to the great ends of improving the health of the country, increasing the produce of the land, and furnishing employment for the people in remunerative works.[57]

With every apology for the length of my communication, which must satisfy you that I have never been an idle man, I remain, sir, your obedient servant,

JOHN MARTIN

[We have great pleasure in inserting this curious and interesting autobiography; but Mr. Martin should be made aware, that we had no intention of sketching the events of his life beyond the appearance of his "Joshua." Whatever our errors may have been (and, by Mr. Martin's own showing, they are neither numerous nor important), we are still very glad that the errors we made in a brief biography of a living artist, should have called forth an account of the artist's own life from his own pen. – ED.]

5
The Deluge 1828
Mezzotint and etching 47.6 × 71.4 cm
The British Museum, London

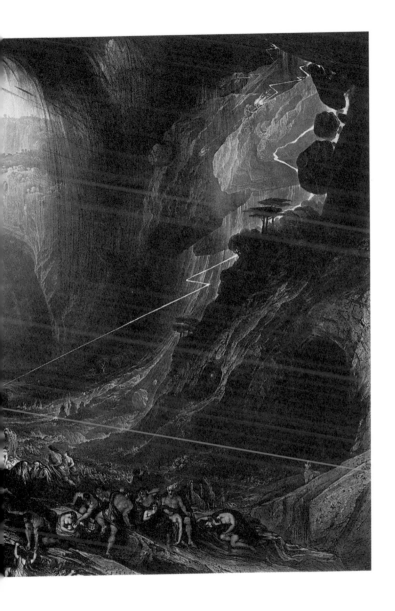

NOTES ON THE TEXTS

1   The British Institution had been founded
in 1805 by a group of collectors and
connoisseurs as an alternative to the artist-run
Royal Academy. It was expressly dedicated
to the promotion of British high art, but
also served to reassert the cultural leadership
of the established social elite. It held two
exhibitions a year: one of contemporary art
and one of Old Masters. See Peter Funnell,
'The London Art World and its Institutions',
in Celina Fox (ed.), *London – World City:
1800–1840*, New Haven and London 1992,
pp.155–66. The British Institution's annual
exhibition of contemporary art opened in
February each year; that of the Royal
Academy, the other major show, in March,
and the Society of British Artists in April.

2   Sir George Beaumont (1753–1827),
art patron and amateur painter. He
commissioned *The Blind Fiddler* (Tate)
from the young Scottish painter David
Wilkie (1785–1841) in 1806. A founding
director of the British Institution, and a
moving force behind the establishment
of the National Gallery, Beaumont was
at the forefront of aristocratic cultural
patronage, although he was also criticised
for his aesthetic conservatism. See Felicity
Owen and David Blayney Brown, *Collector
of Genius: A Life of Sir George Beaumont*,
New Haven and London 1988.

3   No.129 in the exhibition catalogue.
The painting had been commissioned by
Charles Scarisbrick (1800–1860).

4   Martin, as his autobiography makes clear,
was heavily occupied with printmaking and
his engineering speculations since the
1820s, but had recommitted to oil painting
at the end of the 1830s with his large picture

of *The Coronation of Queen Victoria* 1839
(Tate). This had been exhibited at the
London gallery belonging to his friend, the
poet Edwin Atherstone (1788–1872) in
1844, but to little public interest. He had
also exhibited a few substantial subject
paintings, along with landscapes and
watercolours in the London exhibitions
in the mid-1840s but whilst noted (and
often criticised) in the press, these had not
attracted the same level of interest as the
major catastrophe pictures of the 1820s.

5   The same criticism had appeared in the
Lady's Newspaper, 17 February 1849, in
terms that suggested this opinion was
widespread: 'The universal objection to this
clever artist's productions is his colour: it
is cold and disagreeable to the eye'. Whilst
expressing some admiration for the picture,
the *Observer*, 11 February 1849, similarly
complained that 'There is, however,
something not altogether legitimate in
the treatment of this large work, especially
in point of colour. The clouds are inky,
the rocks are inky, the sky, as contra-
distinguished from the clouds, is inky,
and inky is the garb of the rider and the
skin of the horse.' The *Daily News*, 12
February 1849, called it 'cold and inky'.
See also above, p.15.

6   Francis Danby (1793–1861), Irish-born
painter of poetic and sublime landscapes.
These had been linked by critics with
Martin's pictures on the basis of their
intense colours and spectacular treatment
of light effects. At the British Institution
in 1849 Danby exhibited a large picture
of *A Mountain Chieftain's Funeral in Olden
Times* (no.52), which at 157.5 × 203.2 cm

framed was approaching the impressive size of Martin's *Joshua*, and was similarly illustrated by the *Illustrated London News* in its review (17 March 1849, p.177). According to the *Daily News* (12 February 1849) they were 'pitted' against one another on facing walls of the display. A small version of this composition is in the Mellon Collection, Yale Center for British Art, New Haven, and has been compared to Martin's *Pandemonium* (exh. RA 1841) (see Eric Adams, *Francis Danby: Varieties of Poetic Landscape*, exh. cat., Yale Center for British Art, New Haven 1973, no.61) although a closer and more telling comparison may be with the contemporaneous *Arthur and Aegle in the Happy Valley* 1849 (Laing Art Gallery, Newcastle).

7   Henry Nelson O'Neil (1817–1880), Russian-born British painter of painstakingly executed subject pictures. *St Cecilia* and *St Catherine* were nos.211 and 213 in the exhibition, and reproduced along with Martin's *Joshua* in the *Illustrated London News*, 10 March 1849, p.153.

8   First exhibited, to unprecedented popular success, at the British Institution in 1821 (and now in a private collection). See Thomas Balston, *John Martin 1789–1854: His Life and Works*, London 1947, pp.53–65.

9   No.46. Despite the bold description given in the Academy's catalogue for that year, in his 'autobiography' Martin identified the subject of this picture as *Clytie* (see below, p.31).

10 No.363. Now St Louis Art Museum.

11 No.211. Now Glasgow Art Gallery.

12 No.294. These were the lines given by Martin in the exhibition catalogue, taken from the English translation of 'The Transformation of Clytie' by Laurence Eusden (1688–1730), which was included in Samuel Garth's well-known and frequently republished edition of Ovid's *Metamorphoses* (1717).

The large exhibited version of this picture is untraced; a smaller version, dated 1814, and presumably a replica, is in the Laing Art Gallery, Newcastle.

13 Now in National Gallery of Art, Washington, DC. 'Sketch' in this context evidently refers to a first exercise or effort at this subject, rather than a drawing or unfinished piece.

14 Martin sold the painting, together with the large version of *Belshazzar's Feast*, to his former employer William Collins while the 1821 British Institution exhibition featuring the latter was still on. Collins toured the painting relentlessly for the next decade or so, much to his financial benefit, and Martin's chagrin; see above, p.12. Martin gives his title as 'Historical Landscape Painter to Their Royal and Serene Highnesses the Princess Charlotte and Prince Leopold' in the Royal Academy catalogue of 1817.

15 *The Bard* was shown at the Royal Academy in 1817 (no.371) and at the British Institution in 1818 (no.252; now Laing Art Gallery, Newcastle). *Revenge*, based on 'The Passions: An Ode for Music' by the eighteenth-century poet William Collins (1721–1759) appeared at the Royal Academy in 1821 (no.379) and is now lost, although a contemporary report gives a sense of its appearance: 'Mr Martin's Revenge would be effective in company with any standard works ... for it is not, like some of his former pictures, overstrained and inadequately drawn, but is correctly vehement, so that, from the fiercely conflicting passion in the figure of Revenge and the armies fighting under a fiery cope from a town in a state of conflagration, the imagination revels both in the picture's visual and mental powers' (*New Monthly Magazine*, 1 July 1821).

16 An allusion to William Gerard Hamilton MP (1729–1796), who legendarily spoke only once in the House of Commons.

17 These statements are inaccurate. Martin's major exhibits for 1824 were *The Seventh Plague of Egypt* at the Society of British Artists (no.22; Museum of Fine Arts, Boston) and a large picture of *Syrinx* shown at the British Institution (no.238, now untraced). *The Paphian Bower* was first exhibited at the Royal Academy in 1823 (no.427), and was probably later purchased by Charles Scarisbrick, as a painting of that title appeared in the sale of his collection in 1861. It is now untraced, although there are several related paintings and the picture was reproduced in mezzotint. The main authority for Martin's prints are the catalogues accompanying the recent exhibitions based around Michael Campbell's collection: J. Dustin Wees and Michael J. Campbell, *'Darkness Visible': The Prints of John Martin*, Sterling and Francine Clark Art Institute, Williamstown, Massachusetts 1986; Michael J. Campbell with J. Dustin Wees and Richard A. Burnett, *John Martin: Visionary Printmaker*, York Art Gallery 1992; Michael Campbell, *John Martin 1789–1854: La Oscuridad visible*, Calografía Nacional Real Academia de Bellas Artes de San Fernando, Madrid 2006 (with an English translation). The first of these catalogues by Campbell and Wees includes a checklist establishing a numbering system for Martin's prints ('CW' numbers) that has become standard, although the subsequent catalogues contain expanded and additional information. For the print of *The Paphian Bower* by G.H. Phillips (?1800–1852), after Martin, see Campbell 2006, no.33.

18 Martin exhibited four views of Sezincote House in Gloucestershire, a property owned by Sir Charles Cockerell (1755–1837) and recently redesigned in a pseudo-Indian style (reflecting Cockerell's experience working for the East India Company), at the Royal Academy in 1818 (nos.510, 557, 602, 606). A series of ten *Views of Sezincote House* etched by Martin were published in the same year (CW10–19; see Campbell 2006, nos.16–26).

19 A large painting (213.4 × 287 cm framed) exhibited at the British Institution in 1826 (no.63), and engraved in mezzotint by Martin in 1828 (CW78).

20 William Hogarth (1697–1764); George Romney (1734–1802); William Blake (1757–1827); George Morland (1763–1804); George Henry Harlow (1787–1819); Richard Parkes Bonington (1802–1828); Henry Liverseege (1803–1832). The claim about the high prices fetched by their pictures at this date appears to be sound. Hogarth's *Westminster Election* had sold for £200 at Christie's on 28 June 1845; Romney's *Lady Hamilton as Cassandra* had sold for £90 in 1848. Works by Liverseege had sold for up to £94 at Christie's on 6 June 1840, and paintings by Morland went frequently through from the auction houses in the 1840s for prices of £200 or more, whilst Bonington's works (presumably watercolours and small paintings) went for up to £50. Data gleaned from Algernon Graves, *Art Sales from Early in the Eighteenth Century to Early in the 20th Century (Mostly Old Masters and Early English Pictures)*, 3 vols., London 1918.

21 Francis Wheatley (1747–1801), Mary Moser (1744–1819) and Angelica Kauffman (1741–1807) were among the first members of the Royal Academy; Henry Howard (1769–1847) had been Professor of Painting from 1833. The data compiled by Graves (as at note 20, above) indicates the low values fetched by their works. A group of studies by Howard sold at Christie's on 17 March 1849 for around £10 each; a presumably more substantial *Peasant Girl* had still only fetched £31 in 1840. Following the information compiled by Graves, Moser's works do not seem to have appeared on the market at all, whilst works by

Kauffman were absent from the London auction houses from 1838 to 1855 and pictures by Wheatley were similarly out of sight between 1809 and 1879. On the other hand, the major picture by Martin that was auctioned at this time, *The Destruction of Pompeii and Herculaneum*, sold from the London house of the Duke of Buckingham by Christie's on 27 March 1848, went for £105, although it had been commissioned from the artist for 800 guineas. This disparity drew notice in Henry Rumsey Forster's *The Stowe Catalogue Priced and Annotated*, [London] 1848, 21st day's sale, and in the press, for instance, the *Lady's Newspaper*, 1 April 1848.

22 These were the lines of scripture provided by Martin for the catalogue entry of the work in the exhibition catalogue, with a reference to Joshua 10.10–12.

23 By the terms of his will of 1685 the Revd John Shaftoe set up a charity (which continues today) to fund a grammar school in Haydon Bridge. This was free to local boys and girls, and provided lessons in reading, writing, arithmetic, Greek, Latin and geography. See L.C. Coombes, *Shaftoe Trust School, Haydon Bridge, Northumberland and the Rev. John Shaftoe's Charity, 1697–1962*, Hexham 1981.

24 Leonard Wilson, listed as 'coach-maker, High Friar-street' in *The Directory for the Year 1801 of the Town and County of Newcastle upon Tyne, Gateshead, and Places Adjacent*, Newcastle 1801, reprinted Newcastle 2000.

25 Boniface Musso (c.1758–after 1805) was an Italian artist working in London since before 1779, and in Newcastle since around 1790, where he set up as the leading drawing master, and also taught fencing and Italian. His son Charles Muss (1779–1824) moved to London in 1800 and exhibited as an enamel painter before, as noted in Martin's account, turning to china-painting, in which trade he set up in business in 1807.

See Marshall Hall, *The Artists of Northumbria*, new edn, Bristol 2005, and L.H. Cust, 'Muss, Charles (1779–1824)', revised by Alexander Koller, in *Oxford Dictionary of National Biography*, Oxford 2004; online edn, January 2008 <http://www.oxforddnb.com/view/article/19678> (accessed 26 November 2010).

26 A sole surviving painted ceramic of c.1807 with John Martin's initials apparent is in the collection of Michael Campbell, and is illustrated in Campbell 2006, no.1. A second piece previously in the collection of the Victoria and Albert Museum, London, is now lost.

27 Susan Garrett (?1780–1858) of Crondall, Hampshire, whose parents were apparently known to the Muss family. Her exact age is uncertain, although most accounts suggest she was a few years older than John Martin. See Mary Pendered, *John Martin, Painter: His Life and Times*, London 1923, pp.53–4 and Balston 1947, pp.27–8. The marriage produced eight children, born between 1812 and 1825, two of whom died in infancy. Of the surviving children, Isabella (1812–1879) remained unmarried and served as John Martin's personal assistant; Alfred (1814–1872) worked with his father as a mezzotint engraver, but later joined the Tax Office; Zenobia (1816–1902) married the writer Peter Cunningham, who has been identified as the author of the offending biography of Martin reprinted here (see above, p.6); Leopold Charles Martin (1817–1889) worked as a civil servant and wrote an important anecdotal account of his father, published in parts in the *Newcastle Weekly Chronicle* in 1888; Charles (1820–1906) became a successful portrait painter; Jessie (1825–1859) married the sculptor and Egyptologist Joseph Bonomi (1796–1878).

28 Although in the 1811 Royal Academy exhibition catalogue he gives his address as '8 Thanet Place', which may suggest an

additional, if temporary, residence. The later move to Lindsey House, Chelsea, put Martin at the fore of the artistic migration into the borough after around 1850. See 'Settlement and Building: Artists and Chelsea', in Patricia E.C. Croot (ed.), *A History of the County of Middlesex: Volume 12. Chelsea*, London 2004, pp.102–6.

29 William Collins (c.1780–?c.1840), glass painter, based at 227 The Strand, London. His trade card of c.1815 (British Museum, London) announces the 'Gallery of Stain'd & Painted Glass' at that address, and refers to Collins as 'Glass Manufacturer to Her Majesty & the Royal Family'. Among his surviving works are: the painted glass copies of Raphael's *St Paul Preaching at Athens* at the Victoria and Albert Museum, London and the Stained Glass Museum, Ely; a window of 1829–32 in the Sir John Soane Museum, London; and a vividly designed stained-glass window based on Danby's *Opening of the Sixth Seal* still in the parish church of St Andrews, Redbourne, North Lincolnshire. He was still active c.1840, when he produced drawings for a new window in Westminster Abbey ('Modern Glass-Painting', *Art Journal*, vol.2, 1840, p.187).

30 Henry Tresham (c.1750–1814), Irish history painter and briefly Professor of Painting at the Royal Academy in 1807–9.

31 Listed as no.46, 'Landscape: Composition' in the catalogue of the 1811 exhibition. It was one of 212 pictures listed as appearing in the Great Room, the main exhibition space at the Royal Academy at Somerset House. Pictures shown in the Great Room were much more likely to obtain critical and popular attention, and artists who found their works exhibited in the smaller spaces (the Inner Room and the Ante-Room, and the Library and Plaster Academy downstairs) often complained of being slighted. See David H. Solkin (ed.), *Art on the Line: The Royal Academy Exhibitions at Somerset House 1780–1836*, New Haven and London 2001.

32 No.363. Now St Louis Art Museum.

33 Martin had provided a version of this story in a shorter autobiographical letter to the *Athenaeum* in 1834 (14 June 1834, p.459). The story resurfaced in the *Athenaeum* (18 January 1879, p.96) where it is connected, tellingly, with the 'amusement' of a picture by Whistler being hung upside-down: 'When John Martin had finished his well-known "Zadak in Search of the Waters of Oblivion," which was more than once engraved, he sent for a frame-maker's men to frame it, and, having occasion to remain in a room adjoining his studio while they were in the latter room, he was edified by a loud dispute between the men as to which was the top and which the bottom of this picture'. Martin's painting is thus positioned as a distinctly 'modern' work of art, which challenges in some way a traditional understanding of perspectival space.

34 William Manning (1763–1835), Member of Parliament and merchant, with investments and property in the West Indies. He was Governor of the Bank of England from 1812 to 1814.

35 *The Expulsion* was listed as 5'9" × 8' [175.3 × 243.8 cm] (framed) in the British Institution catalogue of 1813, and is now untraced, although the smaller and perhaps unfinished canvas of the same subject in the Laing Art Gallery, Newcastle, may be a version of the composition. Martin referred to the original picture being 'in my own possession' in 1834 (*Athenaeum*, 14 June 1834, p.459). *Adam's First Sight of Eve* was no.211 at the Royal Academy in 1813. Martin, in 1834, says that it was sold to 'Mr Spong' for 70 guineas. The picture is now in the collection of the Glasgow Art Gallery.

36 No.294, in the Ante-Room. According to a note on one of the drawers in the cabinet that Martin used to store his designs and published proposals (Laing Art Gallery, Newcastle) this composition was later

44

altered to the subject of Alpheus and Arethusa. This picture was exhibited at the British Institution in 1833 (no.118) and subsequently sold to Charles Grey, 2nd Earl Grey (1764–1845) (private collection).

37 *Joshua Commanding the Sun to Stand Still upon Gibeon* (National Gallery of Art, Washington, DC) was exhibited in the Ante-Room of the Royal Academy in 1816 (no.347) and at the British Institution in 1817 (no.152).

38 John Fisher (1748–1825), Bishop of Salisbury, was appointed tutor to Princess Charlotte Augusta of Wales (1796–1817) in 1805 and continued in this role until 1817. Fisher was closely connected with the London art world, being chaplain to the Royal Academy and a founder member of the British Institution, although his relationship with Charlotte was not perhaps easy. See *Autobiography of Miss Cornelia Knight, Lady Companion to the Princess Charlotte of Wales* (2 vols.), London 1861, vol.1, p.233: 'His best accomplishment was a taste for drawing, and a love of the fine arts. I have often put him in a good humour by showing him a drawing, or forwarding his proposals of accompanying Princess Charlotte to exhibitions. Indeed, though she was not fond of the Bishop's company at any time … she would good-naturedly allow him to be our cicerone on these occasions'. Charlotte married, in 1816, Prince Leopold of the Belgians (1790–1865), who had met and befriended John Martin while they were briefly neighbours in Marylebone in 1814. Leopold and Charlotte subsequently appointed Martin their official 'Historical Landscape Painter' (see above, note 14).

39 It is unclear what Martin is referring to as 'immediately profitable' tasks, although his views of Sezincote House were published in this year and could be considered as being of this nature (see above, note 18). Martin's move in 1818 to 30 Allsop Terrace was facilitated by a loan provided by his patron William Manning (see above, note 34). This remained his address until 1848.

40 Exhibited at the British Institution in 1819, no.176 (now private collection).

41 No.141 in the British Institution exhibition of 1820, listed as 5'8" × 8' [172.7 × 243.8 cm] (framed), now untraced; it was engraved by Thomas Lupton (1791–1873) in 1828 (Campbell 2006, no.200).

42 The picture was reportedly such a popular success at the British Institution that barriers had to be introduced to protect it from the pressing crowds. The exhibition was extended by two weeks to accommodate the crowds, and the Institution made more than £1,000 in additional ticket and catalogue sales during this extended run. Martin had asked the directors for a pamphlet detailing the picture to be available in the exhibition but they refused this request, presumably lest it set a precedent to other artists and compete with their own standard catalogue. This original pamphlet may be identified with the four-page booklet held in the library the British Museum Prints and Drawings Room (M.M.9–1), and inscribed 'first plate', apparently by Martin. They did, however, elect subsequently to give Martin a special 'gift' of £200 in recognition of his outstanding achievement. See National Art Library, MSL/1941/680, f.86–86v and f.93v. The 'Premiums' had been awarded in earlier years in the Institution's competitions for historical painting.

43 The painting was exhibited as the centrepiece of Martin's solo exhibition at the Egyptian Hall in Piccadilly in 1822, with an accompanying pamphlet and key. The picture had been commissioned by Richard Temple-Nugent-Brydges-Chandos-Grenville, 1st Duke of Buckingham and Chandos (1776–1839) and was first displayed at Stowe before being moved by his heir to Buckingham House in Pall Mall. It was sold in London in 1848 for an

extremely low price, and passed to the National Gallery in 1869, but was lent to Manchester City Art Gallery before being transferred to the Tate Gallery. Here it was kept in store until it was severely damaged in the flood of the gallery's basement in 1928 and written off. Following restoration, it will be redisplayed in 2011.

44 *The Seventh Plague of Egypt* (Museum of Fine Arts, Boston), first shown at the Society of British Artists in 1824; *The Paphian Bower* was shown at the Royal Academy (no.427) in 1823 and is untraced (see above, note 17).

45 *The Creation* was a large painting exhibited at the Society of British Artists in 1825 (no.226), and is untraced, although Martin's mezzotints for *Paradise Lost*, created in 1824, relate closely to this composition (Balston 1947, pp.80–1; CW41). *The Deluge* was first exhibited at the British Institution in 1826. It is now untraced. *The Fall of Nineveh* was first exhibited in a private exhibition run by Martin in 1828 at the Western Exchange, Old Bond Street. The picture was recorded in the Egyptian royal collection in the 1960s, and is now untraced.

46 Martin was commissioned by the publisher Septimus Prowett in 1823 to produce a series of mezzotint illustrations for *Paradise Lost*. Martin received 2,000 guineas for the first twenty-four plates, and a further 1,500 guineas at the end of 1824 for a second series on a smaller format. These became spectacularly successful, and have long been admired as Martin's central artistic achievement. See CW26–49 and 50–73. The engraving of *Belshazzar's Feast* was announced in 1826, and plunged the artist into a legal battle. Collins, the owner of the picture, claimed that the painter had agreed contractually that no such print would be issued until after he himself had issued a reproduction. Martin contested this claim, and his print, engraved on steel, was

published 1 June 1826. Such was the success of the print that the plate was re-engraved and the print reissued in 1832. See Campbell 2006, nos.40–1. Collins's legal case against Martin is in the National Archives, Kew (C13/2017/22), and was reported in the *Examiner*, 23 April 1826, which states Martin's defence. *Joshua* was published in 1827, and *The Deluge* in 1828 (CW77 and CW82), although an etching of the former was recorded in the sale catalogue of Charles Muss's collection in 1824, apparently confirming Martin's claim that he had begun this print in 1823 (CW20, untraced; see Campbell 2006, no.101).

47 Martin is presumably suggesting that he had only one of the large exhibited oil paintings still in his possession, although we cannot be certain to which work he is referring as there are several candidates. *The Deluge* and *Fall of Nineveh* had failed to sell at the time of their exhibition. The latter painting, and the large 1834 version of *The Deluge* (now Yale Center for British Art, New Haven) were bought by Charles Scarisbrick, as was *The Coronation of Queen Victoria* (Tate), although the date of their purchase is not certain. A painting titled 'The Bowers of Bliss' also included in this sale was probably *The Paphian Bower*, exhibited in 1823. *Macbeth*, a large picture that Martin considered important, was still in his studio in 1831, and may still have been with him in 1849. Similarly, the large *Expulsion*, first exhibited in 1813, was still with him in 1834 (see above, note 35).

48 Henry Philip Hope (d.1839), a member of the hugely wealthy banking family, bought *The Fall of Babylon* (1819; private collection); Richard Temple-Nugent-Brydges-Chandos-Grenville, 1st Duke of Buckingham and Chandos (1776–1839), commissioned *The Destruction of Pompeii and Herculaneum* (1822; Tate); John Fleming Leicester, 1st Baron De Tabley

(1762–1827) commissioned a smaller replica of the same picture (1826; Tabley House, Knutsford); John George Lambton, 1st Earl of Durham (1792–1840) bought *The Seventh Plague of Egypt* in 1825 (1823; Museum of Fine Arts, Boston); Charles Grey, 2nd Earl Grey (1764–1845), Prime Minister 1830–4, purchased *Alpheus and Arethusa* (1814–32; private collection); George Granville Sutherland-Leveson-Gower, 2nd Duke of Sutherland (1786–1861), bought *The Assuaging of the Waters* (1840; Fine Arts Museums of San Francisco), although surviving correspondence (Staffordshire and Stoke-on-Trent Archive Service) indicates that the commission was directly managed by his wife, Harriet Sutherland-Leveson-Gower (1806–1868), 2nd Duchess of Sutherland; Prince Albert of Saxe-Coburg-Gotha (1819–1861), Prince Consort of Queen Victoria, purchased the partner picture, *The Eve of the Deluge* in 1841 (1840; Royal Collection); Charles Scarisbrick was, as noted above (p.12), Martin's most extensive single patron.

49 Martin's apparently homemade cabinet (Laing Art Gallery, Newcastle) incorporated a set of small drawers designed for these and other honours, each carefully labelled with their contents.

50 Martin was a key witness at the Select Committee on Arts and Manufactures of 1835–6, which had been set up with the intention of exposing the corrupt, 'aristocratic', self-interest of the London art establishment. See Tom Gretton, '"Art Is Cheaper in France and Goes Deeper": The Language of the Parliamentary Select Committee on Art and Design 1835–36', in Andrew Hemingway and William Vaughan (eds.), *Art in Bourgeois Society 1790–1850*, Cambridge 1998, pp.84–100; Jane Alexander Webb, 'An Analysis of the Select Committee on Arts and Manufactures of 1835–6: Anatomy, Benthamism and

Design', PhD Thesis, University of Wolverhampton 2003. In his evidence, Martin was careful not to condemn the Academicians as such, only the closed nature of the institution: 'In speaking against the academy, I wish it to be understood to apply to the system, and not to the individuals, for I am proud to reckon amongst my friends the most distinguished members of the body'.

51 The issue of artistic copyright exercised Martin throughout his career, with the artist insisting in various contexts to the rights of artists to commercially exploit images of their own invention. In 1826, William Collins applied for an injunction in an attempt to stop Martin producing an engraving of his own painting *Belshazzar's Feast* (see above, note 46). In 1833, Martin took the proprietors of an exhibition at the Queen's Bazaar in London to court, claiming that their panoramic version of *Belshazzar's Feast* was a damaging infringement of his copyright (the case was dismissed; see 'Court of Chancery', *Morning Chronicle*, 29 July 1833). He was acutely aware of the continuing commercial exploitation of his images by other publishers and artists, in Britain and abroad, who issued unlicensed versions and adaptations of his major compositions. In fact he set up a printing press in his own house to try to prevent piracy, 'having suffered immensely from this sort of thing' (John Martin to George Linnecar, 24 August 1834, National Art Library, MSL/1979/7461/31A).

52 Martin had listed his various published plans in his *Thames and Metropolis Improvement Plan* (1849), and this forms the basis of the listing provided by Balston (Balston 1947, App.5b). Referred to here are: *Plan for Supplying the Cities of London and Westminster with Pure Water from the River Colne*, London 1827 (untraced; see Balston 1947, App.5b, no.1);

Mr John Martin's Plan for Supplying with Pure Water the Cities of London and Westminster, and of Materially Improving and Beautifying the Western Parts of the Metropolis, London 1828; a 'second edition' is the earliest known, and presumably revises and expands the previous *Plan*; see Balston 1947, App.5b, no.2; also Campbell 2006, nos.44–5. For an overview of Martin's plans and inventions see Balston 1947, pp.120–32, and for his plans for London see also Felix Barker and Ralph Hyde, *London as it Might Have Been*, London 1982, pp.86–9.

53 'Second Plan for Supplying London with Purer Water' and 'Plan for More Effectively Draining Certain Marshy Land Contiguous to the Thames' appeared as Sections VI–VII of *Outlines of Several New Inventions for Maritime and Inland Purposes*, London 1829 (Balston 1947, App.5b, no.3).

54 See Balston 1947, App.5b, nos.4 (1832), 6 (1834), 9 (1842), and 12 (1847). The 1836 plan referred to here is known only from a reprint of a later date (see Balston 1947, p.274); *The Thames and Metropolis Plan First Division* (Balston 1947, App.5b, no.11) is dated 1846 but like others of these publications might have appeared earlier than the stated date, and thus may be the publication for '1845' mentioned by Martin. The *Report on the Select Committee on Metropolis Improvements*, published in 1838, includes diagrams of Martin's proposed embankment of the Thames, which incorporated sewers.

55 Martin is certainly overstating his influence and his isolation in this regard. The Public Health Act of 1848 established a General Board of Health, although with limited powers, a development which is usually attributed to long-term agitation from the social reformer Edwin Chadwick (1800–1890) and the impact of the massive cholera epidemic of 1847–8.

56 The report of the Royal Commission on Metropolitan Railway Termini (1846) recommended that new railways should not be allowed to enter the City or West End; as a result the mainline termini were established in a ring around the heart of London. Martin's own proposals for London's rail system were dismissed as unrealistic. See Barker and Hyde 1982, p.134.

57 *Plan of the London Connecting Railway & Railway Transit along Both Banks of the Thames*, lithograph published 1845 (Balston 1947, App.5b, no.10; Campbell 2006, no.46). Several of the inventions listed here appeared together in *Outlines for New Inventions for Maritime and Inland Purposes*, London 1829 (Balston 1947, App.5b, no.3), and Martin appeared before the Select Committee on Accidents in Mines in 1835, publishing his own plans for ventilating coal mines in 1835 and 1849 (Balston 1947, App.5b, nos.8, 14).